ANGLO SAXON MAP OF OLD ENGLAND 700 AD

THE NATIONAL COUNCIL FOR METAL DETECTING'S

CODE OF CONDUCT

FOR RESPONSIBLE DETECTOR USERS

Do not trespass. Ask permission before venturing on to any private land.

Respect the country code. Do not leave gates open when crossing fields. Do not damage crops or frighten animals.

Do not leave a mess. it is perfectly simple to extract a coin or other small object buried a few inches under the ground without digging a large hole. Use a sharpened trowel or knife to cut a neat flap. Do not remove the plug of earth entirely from the ground. remove the object. replace the soil and grass carefully and even you would have difficulty finding the same spot again.

Help to keep Britain tidy….and help yourself. bottle tops, silver paper and cans are the last things you should throw away. you might well be digging them up the following year. Do yourself and the community a favour by taking the rusty iron and junk you find to the nearest litter bin.

If you discover any live ammunition or any lethal objects such as an unexploded bomb or mine. Do not touch it. Mark the spot carefully and report the find to the local police and landowners

Familiarize yourself with the law relating to archaeological sites. Remember it is illegal to use a metal detector on an ancient monument unless you are granted permission. Report all finds.

You are an ambassador to the hobby so be responsible.

Introduction

This book has been compiled due to Archaeologists, Detectorists and historians showing such a keen interest where the dark age period is concerned. I have hear so many people saying 'oh 'you cant get those good books no more, They were deleted 40 years ago. If it wasn't for those early archaeologists of the 1800s carrying out all those excavations through years of searching and logging all their research down then our past history would have a large hole in it today. Detectorists, historians and archaeologist would be still searching today for what was found back then, Instead of this we can now concentrate on making new discoveries, we are now 150 years in front instead of behind.

It is very important not to forget todays archaeologists who are constantly restricted to tiny budgets which only allow for 3 digs per year if lucky. Since the 1950s to present, Archaeologists have discovered thousands of new sites. Detectorists have discovered thousands of new sites along with millions of important finds, then the historian who spends year upon year writing and field walking.

This book contains many of those past and present saxon sites which were discovered by endless work on behalf of the archaeologists from the 1800s to the present. It also contains many sites discovered by detectorists from the 1970s to the present during endless searching in all kinds of bad weather. Due to the contents of this book, I will have to make it clear that lots of these sites will be out of bounds scheduled for digs or listed as monumental, the land owner might not want to give you permission either.

It is very important that prior to detecting, you find out if you are legally allowed to detect on that land that you wish to go on. It is also important to note, that walking the field, collecting all the pottery from it then storing it in your shed for years and not reporting it is frowned upon. The first thing detectorists look for is pottery, This can give valuable information on the history of that field, 'Remember don't remove pottery just for the sake of it, leave it were it is, what might look like a piece of modern red roof tile to one person might be a piece of roman villa roof tile. what might look 100 years old might be 1700 years old. 'Dont forget the advice.

Whatever your interest in history, I hope this gazetteer helps you in some way, I have listed as many sites as possible with full grid references so that those sites are easy to find, some sites now may no longer exist due to house builds but most will remain untouched so good hunting, excavating, fieldwalking.

Contents

Northumbrian Kings

Down to the year 729

Deira	Woden	Bernicia
Wegdaeg		Baeldaeg
Siggar		Bernie
Swaebdaeg		Wegbrand
Siggeot		Ingibrand
Saebald		Alusa
Saefugal		Angengeot
Soemel		Ethelbert
Uestoruacna		Oessa
Uilgils		Eoppa
Uuscfrea		Ida
Yffi		Adda-Theoric
Aella		Ethelric
[560-90]		
Edwin	Aelfric	Ethelfrith
		[593-616]
	Osric	Eanfrith
		[632-3]

	Oswine	St Oswald
	[644-51]	
		Oswiu
		[641-70]
Ethelwald		Egfrith
[651-4]		[670-85]
		Aldfrith
		[685-704]
		Osred I
		[705-16]
		Osric
		[718-29]

The Kingdom was passed down to other families during the 8th century.It lasted until 878 AD where the Vikings raided

Mercia

Woden

Watholgeot

Uihtlaeg

Uermund

Offa

Angengeot

Eamer

Icil

Cnebba

Cynwald

Creoda

Pyba

Penda

[632-54]		Eowa		Coenwalh
			Osmund	
		Alwih	Eanulf	Cundwalh
Wulfhere	Ethelred		Thinefrith	Centwine
[657-74]				Cynreou

Coenred   Coelred

[704-9]   [709-16]

                        Ethelbald   Bassa

                        [716-757]

                                    Offa   Cuthbert

                                    [757-96]

                                    Ecgfrith

                                    [796]

                        Coenwulf   Ceolwulf

                        [796-821]   [821-23]

Wessex

Woden

Baeldaeg

Brond

Gewis

Elesa

Cerdic

[534]

Crenda

Cynric

[534-60]

Ceawlin				Cutha
[560-91]		Ceol		Ceolwulf
	Cenbehrt	[591-7]		[597-611]
Cuthwine		Cyngelis		Cuthgils
		[611-43]		
Cuthwulf				Cenferth
[Cutha]				
Ceolwald	Caedwalla	Cenwalh	Centwine	Cenfus
	[685-8]	[643-74]		

Cenred   Aescwine

                                                                [674-6]

        Ine   Inglid

    [688-726]

                     Eoppa

                     Eafa

                     Ealhmund

                     Egbert

                     [802-89]

                     Athelwulf

                     [839-55]

Athelstan   Ethelbald   Ethelbert   Burgred   Alred

   [850]   [855-60]   [860-6]   [King of Mercia]   [871-99]

                                                 Edward The Elder

                                                    [899-925]

             Athelstan   Edmund   Eadred

             [925-75]   [939-46]   [939-55]

Eadwig   Edgar

[955-9]   [959-75]

Edward The Martyr   Richard I   Swein

[975-8]   [Duke Of Normandy]   [1014]

Ethelred Unraed-Emma Cnut-Aelfgifu Of Northampton

[978-1016]

Edmund Ironside   Edward   Harthacnut   Swein

The Confessor   [1040-2]   King Of Norway

[1042-66]   Harold I

[1035-40]

A Succession Of Norman Kings Followed The Saxon Period

East Yorkshire & The Wolds

Acklam   Anglo Saxon Inhumation Cemetery   SE 792612

Appleton Le Street   [Anglo Saxon Burial [Female] SE 733357147

            [Gold Earings/Amber Necklace]

Boynton   Anglo Saxon Settlement Site   TA 130677

Bulmer   2 Anglo Saxon Cruciform Brooches   No Grid

Caythorpe   Anglo Saxon Settlement Site   TA 12456742

Driffield   Anglo Saxon Hut Site & Inhumation TA 04165782

            Cemetery Known as Cheesecake Hill

            Tumulus with Amber beads &

            Cruciform Brooches

Driffield   Anglo Saxon Cemetery Known as Moot TA02355830

            Hill-Sword & Spearheads Found-Many

            Skeletons minus Grave goods

Elmswell   Anglian Settlement Site with many   TA 000577

            Finds of Saxon & other periods-Site of

            Major importance

Etton	Anglo Saxon Inhumation Cemeteries	SE 952428
	Covering large area-Skeletons &	SE 954428
	Tweezers found	SE 958428
		SE 962428
Folkton	Anglian well Settlement Site	TA041767
Garton	Anglo Saxon Inhumation Cemetery	SE 95666181
Goodmanham	Saxon Royal Centre &Pagan	No Grid
	Temple here-Not yet Found-	
	Rep to have belonged to Cofi the	
	High priest in the early 7th century	
	Criciform & square headed found	
Hayton	Anglo Saxon Settlement Site on the	SE 818456
	Roman Fort	

[No Go Area Be warned]

[Hayton]

| **Hornsea** | Anglo Saxon Inhumation Cemetery | TA 207484 |

Kilham	Anglo Saxon Inhumation Cemetery 144 Relics found	TA 07926593
Kilham	Anglo Saxon Settlement Site Annular & Pins found	TA 07786593
Kilham	Anglo Saxon Burial Site 6th Cent Middle Street	TA 063643
Kilham	Anglo Saxon Burial Site South Of Kilham Grange Farm	TA 079660
Kirkburn	Anglian Burial Containing 6 Spearheads	SE 978579
Kirkby U	Anglian Cemetery on 2 Bronze Age Barrows	SE 822594
Londesborough	Anglian ornaments with Grave goods	SE 871462

Nafferton	Anglian Occupation Site	TA 060587
Nunburnholme	Anglian Inhumation Cemetery E of Garforth Farm	SE 864489
Rudston	Anglo Saxon Settlement Site with 2 Cruciform Brooches & Spears	TA 116671
Sancton	Anglo Saxon Cemetery –Several Hundred burials many relics & Brooches	SE 9034 03
Seamer	Anglian Inhumation Cemetery- Gold pendants-Knives-2 gold rings- 2 gold beads-2 gold pins set in garnets- 3 gold tabs set in garnets-1 silver ring- 1 silver annular-silver wire beads & jet Ring all found on site	TA 02838417
Seamer	Anglian hut site crossgates	TA 032833

Ullrome	Saxon & Danish burial site	TA 132577
Walkington	Anglo Saxon burial site	SE 96253568
Whatton	Anglo Saxon nunnery on sit	TA 023499
	Known as wetadun-AD 704-5	
	Later known as Whatton priory-	
	Many brooches & rings found	
W.Heslerton	Anglo Saxon Inhumation Cemetery	SE 917766
Willerby	Anglo Saxon Inhumation Cemetery	TA 0228793

A Summary Of Coins Found At Newbald Productive Site

Eadberht [738-757]	**Archbishop Ecgberht [734-766]**	**11**
Eadberht [738-757]	**Class A**	**6**
	Class B	**5**
	Class C	**1**
	Class D	**4**
	Class E	**5**
	Class F	**2**
	Class G	**1**
Alchred [705-774]	**Animal Type**	**3**
Aethelred I 1st Reign [774-779	**Animal Type**	**1**
Aelfwald I [779-788]	**Animal Type**	**3**

Aethelred I 1ˢᵗ Reign Or 2ⁿᵈ Reign [789-796] with

Archbisop Eanbald I [778-796]   1

Aethelred I 2ⁿᵈ Reign [789-796] Moneyers Type   6

Aelfwald II [806?-808?] [Or Aelfwald I ?]   3

Eanred [810-841?] Phase 1 A Base Silver   10

Phase 2 Copper Alloy   5

Aethelred II [841-?-844?] [844-849?]   27

Archbishop Wigmund [837?-854?]   10

Osberht [849?-867?   9

Lincolnshire

Asgarby	Anglo Saxon Burial Site	TF 335667
Barton	Anglo Saxon Monastery & Burial site founded by king Wulfere in 669-72-Danes Destroyed it in 870- 7 gold Rings found with skeletons & weapons	SE 07362169 SE 073217
Branston	Anglo Saxon Spearhead	TF 025682
Bunwell	Anglo Saxon Domestic Site	TM 129932
Barton U Stather	Anglo Saxon burials	SE 904171
Caistor	Anglo Saxon burials in Bronze age barrow	SK 97038896

Castle Dyke South Anglo Saxon Inhumation   TA 03172175

Cemetery-gold beads &

Silver buckle-bronze wire

Bronze bracelet-bronze

Workbox-beaten bronze

Hanging bowl-short sword

& beads-scales & weights

Coleby   Anglo Saxon Inhumation   SK 980601

Cemetery-rings-glass beads

Brooches & lots of weapons

Elsham   Anglo Saxon Cemetery-500   TA 046125

Burials discovered

Fillingham   Anglo Saxon Settlement   SK 970865

Long brooch found

Flixborough	Anglo Saxon Settlement	SE 88921467
	2 cruciform brooches	
Flixborough	Anglo Saxon guilded	SE 877142
	Bronze disc brooch	
Glentham	Anglo Saxon cruciform	TF 01809195
	Brooch found	
Grayingham	Anglo Saxon burials	SE 935962
Hatton	Anglo Saxon brooches	TF 182764
Hibaldstowe	Anglo Saxon Inhumations	SE 94050135
	Sword & scabbard-bridle	
	Bits-2 knives-socketed	
	Spear & grave goods	

Irby On Humber	Anglo Saxon Burial	TA 217042
	Grounds spread over a	
	Gravel spur on a hill	
	Grave goods & stray	
	Finds include gilted	
	Bronze great square	
	Headed brooch-girdle	
	Hangers-cruciform-	
	Guilded spiral saucer	
	Brooches-sleeve clasps	
	Silver serpent finger rings	
	Silver braceaes-minature	
	Shields-knives-spear heads-	
	Keys-6th cent site known as	
	Wellbeck hill	
Kirmington	Saxon cruciform-strapends &	TA 095174
	Buckles-vast amounts of finds	
	From all other early periods	

Kirton/Lindsey	Anglo Saxon Cemetery	SK 938007
Laceby	Anglo inhumation cemetery	TA 20340662
	3 cruciform-2 sq headed	
	Knobbled ring-annular	TA 20470667
	Brooch-spiral pin-knife &	
	Beads	
Little Hale	Anglo Saxon Cemetery	TA 159412
Maidenwell	Saxon bronze bucket	TF 319785
Manton	Anglo saxon settlement	SE 93430470
Manton	Anglo saxon cemetery	SE 942042
Messingham	Anglian hut sites-	SE 91040340
	Cruciform brooches-	
	Ceramic beads-other finds	SE 90800390
Nettleton	Anglo saxon inhumation	TA 11080058
	Cemetery	

Owesby	Anglo saxon cruciform	TF 05899492
Partney	Anglo saxon inhumations In round barrow	TF 42256810
Quarrington	Anglo saxon industrial sites	TF 05814457 TF 040430
Riby	Anglo saxon burials	TA 187079
Saxby	Anglo saxon guilt socketed Spearhead	SK 98568580
Scotter	Anglian knife & scattered Skeletons between river & Graveyard	SE 88680058
Searby	Anglo saxon burials	TA 075060

S Elkington	anglian cremation cemetery	TF 312883
S Ferriby	Anglo saxon cruciforms &	SE 99152169
	Long brooches-vast amounts	
	Of finds from all other	
	Early periods	
Spridlington	Anglo saxon burials	TA 008845
Stenigot	Anglo saxon inhumations	TF 25288208
Tetford	Anglo saxon inhumations	TF 31107620
Waddington	Anglo saxon inhumations	SK 97716398
	Glass beads-brooches-other	
	Bronze objects	
Welbourne	AS burials-brooches	SK 97655304
	Clasps-from temple hill	

W Keal	Anglo saxon cremation cemetery on hall hill	TF 356640
Willoughton	Anglo saxon hut site	SK 933927
Willoughton	Anglo saxon enamelled Brooch & hanging bowl From strawsons hill	SK 73479351
Willoughton	Anglo saxon bronze rim From a bowl -1st temple field	SK 93859280
Winteringham	Sceattas found with Spiral pin & iron knife	SE 93372228 SE935221 SE 934223

Worlaby   Anglo saxon inhumation   TA 017143

Cemetery-silver pendants

Bosses-knives-shield studs

Annulars-bronze buckles-

Amber beads-spearheads

Nottinghamshire

Cotgrave	Anglian burial site	SK 656318
Holme Pierrepoint	Anglo saxon cemetery	SK 625391
Netherfield	Anglian burial site	SK 625410
Newark	Anglian cremation Cemetery fosse way 383 burials recorded	SK 793536
Nottingham	Anglo saxon domestic site	SK 574396
S Muskham	Anglo saxon hut site	SK 798578
Trent Valley	Anglo saxon gold annular Brooch set with garnets	SK 70835999

Norfolk

Bacton	Anglo saxon industrial site	TG 335319
Bale	Anglo saxon burial site	TG 011367
Beechamwell	Anglo saxon burial site	TF 757049
Billingford	Anglo saxon burial site	TG 007203
Brandon	Anglian occupation site	TL 778866
Bridgham	Anglo saxon burial site	TL 939845
Brooke	Anglo saxon cemetery	TM 294995
Broome	Anglo saxon cemetery	TM 346931
Brow Of The Hil	Anglo saxon industrial site	TF 657193

Brow Of The Hill	Anglo saxon settlement	TF 66252079
Brundall	Anglo saxon cemetery	TG 330079
Caistor	Anglo saxon cemetery	TG 235032
Caistor	Anglo saxon cemetery	TG 229039
Castle Acre	Anglo saxon cemetery	TF 797156
Castle Rising	Anglo Saxon domestic site	TF 666246
Catton	Anglo saxon cemtery	TG 227099
Congham	Anglo saxon domestic site	TF 718233
Dersingham	Anglo saxon cemetery	TF 693303

Drayton	Anglo saxon cemetery	TG 188131
Earsham	Anglo saxon cemetery	TM 326888
East Runton	AS Industrial site	T G 183414
Gissing	Anglo saxon burial site	TM151850
Gt Carbrooke	Anglo saxon burial site	TF 951022
Gt Ellingham	Anglo saxon burial site	TM 020973
Grimston	Anglo saxon cemetery	TF 721224
Gt Walsingham	Anglo saxon cemetery	TF928375
Hargham	Anglo saxon cemetery	TM 019913
Hilgay	Anglo saxon burial site	TL 622981

Kenninghall	Anglo saxon cemetery	TM 034861
Kirby Cane	Anglo saxon cemetery	TM 373933
Langhale	AS domestic site	TM 302969
Langham	Anglo saxon burial site	TG 020411
Little Snoring	Anglo saxon cemetery	TF 953322
Little Walsingham	AS burial site	TF 930364
Lynford	Anglo saxon cemetery	TL 822937
Mannington	Anglo saxon cemetery	TG 147323
Mundford	Anglo saxon cemetery	TL 802935
N Elmham	AS Domestic site	TF 987215

N Elmham	Anglo saxon cemetery	TF 983195
N Elmham	AS Industrial site	TF 981195
N Runcton	Anglo saxon burial site	TF 646159
Northwold	Anglo saxon cemetery	TL 770961
Norwich	AS Industrial site	TG 228089
Pensthorpe	Anglo saxon cemetery	TF 950295
Poringland	Anglo saxon cemetery	TG 271020
Postwick	AS Domestic site	TG 300074
Rockland	Anglo saxon cemetery	TL 994948
Sedgeford	Anglo saxon burial site	TF 717357

Shadwell	Anglo saxon cemetery	TL 935834
Shropham	Anglo saxon cemetery	TL 984927
Small Burgh	Anglo saxon burial site	TG 337240
Snettisham	As Domestic site	TF 692332
Southtown	AS Gold tremissis found	TG 499055
Sporle	Anglo saxon cemetery	TF 854075
Stockton	Anglo saxon burial site	TM 387941
Thorpe	Anglo saxon burial site	TG 254087
Tottenhill	Anglo saxon cemetery	TF 635108
Wereham	Anglo saxon burial site	TF 681015

W Runton	Anglo saxon burial site	TG 174417
Witten	Anglo saxon burial sites	TG 337322
		TG 366320
Wormegay	Anglo saxon cemetery	TF 672125
Wretton	Anglo saxon burial site	TF 696007
Wretham	Anglo saxon burial site	TL948898
Yarmouth	Anglo saxon cemetery	TG 518090

Saxon Coins Found In Norfolk

Alby Hill	Offa [dated 767-796]	TG 19 35
Banham	Early continental [dated 675-750]	TM 06 88
	Early continental [dated 675-750]	
Bawdeswell	Edward [dated 1042-66]	TG 03 19
Bexwell	Early continental [dated 675-750]	TF 64 03
Bio Norton	Maurice [dated582-602]	TM 01 78
	Beornwulf [dated823-825]	
	Early continental [dated 675-750]	TM 01 78
Blackborough End	Burgred [dated 852-874]	TF 66 16
Bridgham	Eadmund [dated 855-869]	TL 95 87
	Aethelstan [dated 825-845]	
	Aethelheard [dated 793-805]	

Cnut [dated [dated 1016-35]

Brow

Of The Hill Edward [dated 899-924]   TF 68 19

Early continental [dated 675-750]

Early continental [dated 675-750]

Edward [dated 1042-66]

Eadred [dated 946-955]

Eadberht [dated 796-798

Beonna [dated749-760]

Briston   Early continental [dated 675-750]   TG 06 32

Castle Acre Edward [dated 975-978]   TF 81 15

Edward [dated 1042-66]

Coenwulf [dated 796-821]

Clay   Edward [dated 757-796]   TG 04 43

Next to

The sea

Clint Green	Coenwulf [dated 796-821]	TG 01 10
Colegate End	Edward [dated 1042-66]	TM 19 86
Colkirk	Early continental [dated 675-750] Edgar [dated 959-975]	TF 91 26
Colney	Coenwulf [dated 796-821]	TG 18 07
Cranwich	Edward [dated 975-978]	TL 78 94
Crowshill	Edgar [dated 959-75]	TF 95 07
Croxton	Cnut [dated 1016-35]	TL 90 87
Deopham green	Early continental [dated 675]	TM 05 99
Ditchingham	Aethelstan [dated 825-845]	TM 33 91

Downham Market Aethelred [dated 840-848]   TF 61 03

East Bilney Early continental [dated 675-750]   TF 95 19

East   Early continental [dated 675-750]   TF 92 08

Bradenham   Aldfrif [dated 685-704]

Lucida [dated 826-827]

East Harling Harthacnut [dated 1035-42]   TL 99 86

Beonna [dated749-760]

Harold [dated 1035-40]

Fakenham   Eadwig [dated 955-959]   TF 92 30

Beonna [dated 749-760]

Early continental [dated 675-750]

Foulsham   Edward [dated 975-978]   TG 03 24

Gt

Ryburgh   Early continental [dated 675-750]   TF 95 27

Gunthorpe	Aethelstan [dated 924-939]	TG 01 34
Hales	Carolingian Louis [dated 814-840]	TM 38 98
Hamrow	Aethelred [dated 978-1016]	TF 9123
Hindringham	Offa [dated 757-796]	TF 98 36
	Eadred [dated 946-955]	
Kenninghall	Cnut [dated 1016-35]	TM 03 86
Kings lynn	Early continental [dated 675-750]	TF 61 20
Little Fransham	Early continental [dated 675-750]	TF 90 12
Merton	Aethelred [dated 978-1016]	
	Gold saxon coin [dated 600-675]	

Middle

Harding	Aethelred [dated 978-1016]	TL 98 85
	Edward [dated 1042-66]	
	Berthwulf [dated 840-852]	
	Beonna [dated 749-760]	
Mileham	Aethelheard [dated 793-805]	TF 91 19

North

Lopham	Aethelred [dated 978-1016]	TM 03 83
	Edward [dated 899-924]	
	Ceolnoth [dated 833-870]	
Pott Row	Aethelred [dated 978-1016]	TF 70 22
Pristow green	Carolingian Charles [840-77]	TM 13 89

Quidenham	Aethelred [dated 978-1016]	TM 02 87
	Cnut [dated 1016-35]	
	Edward [dated 1042-66]	
	Berhtwulf [dated 840-852]	

Rockland

St Peter	Early continental [dated 675-750]	TL 98 98
	Aethelred [dated 978-1016]	
	Eanred [dated 810-840]	

Saham

Toney	Gold saxon coin [dated 600-675]	TF 89 02

Silfield	Edward [dated 899-924]	TM 12 98

Sporle	Early continental [dated 675-750[	TF 84 11
	Aethelred [dated 978-1016]	
	Nicephorus [dated 963-969]	

Southery South	Edward [dated 1042-66]	TL 62 94
Pickenham	Corilingian Charles [dated 840-877]	TF 85 04
Stoke Ferry	Aethelred [dated 978-1016]	TF 70 00
	Harthacnut [dated 1035-42]	
	Early continental [dated 675-750]	
	Harold [dated 1035-40]	
	Edward [dated 1042-66]	
	Corilingian Louis [dated 814-840]	
Surlingham	Edward [dated 1042-66]	TG 31 06
Swaffham	Aethelred [dated 978-1016]	TF 81 09
Thompson	Early continental [dated 675-750]	TL 91 96
	Aethelred [dated 978-1016]	
	Offa [dated 757-796]	

Walpole

St Andrew   Edward [dated 1042-66]   **TF 50 16**

Walsoken   Early continental [dated 675-750]   **TF 47 10**

              Cenwulf [dated 796-821]

Watton   Early continental [dated 675-750]   **TF 91 00**

              Coenwulf [dated 796-821]

              Gold Merovingian found [590-670]

West Walton Early continental [dated 675-750] **TF 47 13**

              Aethelred [dated 978-1016]

              Harold [dated 1035-40]

              Edward [dated1042-66]

              Cnut [dated 1016-35]

West Winch   Early continental [dated 675-750] **TF 62 15**

Weybourne   Aethelred [dated 978-1016]   **TG 11 42**

Wormegay   Early continental [dated 675-750] **TF 66 11**

Suffolk

Ashbocking	Anglo saxon Domestic site	TM 175551
Badwell Ash	Anglo saxon cemetery	TM 002693
Bardwell	Anglo saxon burial site	TL 943728
Barham	Anglo saxon cemetery	TM 133515
Barnham Heath	Anglo saxon burial site	TM 887797
Barrow Bottom	Anglo saxon burial site	TL 773661
Botesdale	Anglo saxon industrial site	TM 040750
Botesdale	Anglo saxon settlement Knife found	
Bramford	Anglo saxon burial site	TM 04307600

Brandon	Anglo saxon settlement site	TL 778866
Bungay	Anglo saxon burial site	TM 327879
Bury st Edmunds	Anglo saxon cemetery	TL 845633
Butley	Anglo saxon domestic site	TM 379500
Butley Corner	Anglo saxon industrial site	TM 374528
Chillesford	Anglo saxon burial site	TM 374528
Coddenham	Anglo saxon burial site	TM 115527
Culford	Anglo saxon burial site	TL 833703
Eye	Anglo saxon cemetery	TM 156748
Fakenham	Anglo saxon burial site	TL 906772

Finningham	Anglo saxon burial site	TM 066684
Fornham St Gene	Anglo saxon cemetery	TL 834690
Fornham St Martin	Anglo saxon burial site	TL 846658
Great Thurlow	Anglo saxon burial site	TL 680502
Grimstone End	Anglo saxon Domestic site	TL 935690
Hoxne	Anglo saxon burial site	TM 180775
Ipswich	Anglo saxon cemetery	TM 146445
Ixworth	Anglo saxon cemetery	TL 935701
Ixworth	Anglo saxon burials & huts	TL 936693

Ixworth	Anglo saxon settlement	TL 935692
Ixworth	Anglo saxon burial site	TL 925720
Ixworth Thorpe	Anglo saxon burial site	TL 925720
Kenninghall	Anglo saxon cemetery	TM 034861
Langham	Anglo saxon burial site	TM 978692
Little Bealings	Anglo saxon domestic site	TM 228464
Needham Market	Anglo saxon burial site	TM 079561
Redgrave	Anglo saxon burial site	TM 046787
Rendlesham	Anglo saxon domestic site	TM 340510
Rendlesham	Anglo saxon cemetery	TM 040760

Rickinghall Inf	**Anglo saxon domestic site**	**TM 040760**
Rickinghall Sup	**Anglo saxon domestic site**	**TM 038743**
Risby Heath	**Anglo saxon burial site**	**TL 792685**
Shadwell	**Anglo saxon cemetery**	**TL 935834**
Snape	**Anglo saxon cemetery & Boat burial**	**TM 402593**
Stanton	**Anglo saxon burial site**	**TL 955742**
Thorndon	**Anglo saxon cemetery**	**TM 136701**
Tostock	**Anglo saxon guilt buckle**	**TL 960936**
Wattisfield	**Anglo saxon domestic site**	**TM 006741**

Wattisfield	**Anglo saxon burial site**	**TM005731**
Wickham Mkt	**Anglo saxon burial site**	**TM 302567**
Woodbridge	**Anglo saxon burial site**	**TM 079784**
Wortham	**Anglo saxon burial site**	**TM 079784**

Cambridge

Babraham	Anglo saxon settlement	TL 514494
Barnwell	Anglo saxon cemetery	TL 460580
Barrington	AS cemetery Hoopers field	TL 387497
Barrington	Anglo saxon cemetery	TL 373495
Cambridge	Anglo saxon cemetery	TL 448592
Cambridge	AS burials & brooch	TL 445571
Cambridge	Anglo saxon domestic site	TL 445592
Cherry Hutton	Anglo saxon cemetery	TL 484555
Clayhithe	Anglo saxon settlement	TL 49246417

Foxton	Anglo saxon cemetery	TL 407488
Foxton	Anglo saxon cemetery	TL 407489
Girton	Anglo saxon cemetery	TL 423609
Grantchester	AS domestic & burial site	TL 431556
Harlton	Anglo saxon cemetery	TL 413520
Hauxton	Anglo saxon burial site	TL 432528
Hauxton	Anglo saxon buildings	TL 435524
Little Shelford	Anglo saxon burial site	TL 459509
Milton	Anglo saxon wrist clasps	TL 46356240
Newham	Anglo saxon cemetery	TL 439574

Oakington	Anglo saxon burial site	TL 415645
Sawston	Anglo saxon burial site	TL 48255045
Stow Cum Quy	AS grave & cruciform	TL505595
Waterbeach	Anglo saxon domestic site	TL489656
Waterbeach	Anglo saxon settlement	TL 49326481

Warwickshire

Alcester	Anglo saxon cemetery	SP 086570
Alveston	Anglo saxon domestic site	SP 208548
Alveston	Anglo saxon cemetery	SP 210547
Alveston	As burial & domestic site	SP 213554
Arrow	Anglo saxon burial site	SP 079557
Aston Cantlow	Anglo saxon burial site	SP 134596
Baginton	Anglo saxon domestic site	SP 342747
Baginton	Anglo saxon cemetery	SP 347747
Bascote	Anglo saxon burial site	SP 450636

Bidford

On Avon   Anglo saxon domestic site   SP 099519

Clopton

Meon Hill   Anglo saxon burial site   SP 175454

Emscote   Anglo saxon cemetery   SP 206652

Eynesbury

Conygeer   Anglo saxon burial site   SP 188595

Halford Bridge   Anglo saxon cemetery   SP 259453

Hatton Rock   Anglo saxon domestic site   SP 237577

Little Rollright   Anglo saxon cemetery   SP 295309

Long Itchington   Anglo saxon burial site   SP 414658

Marton	Anglo saxon cemetery	SP 404681
Napton Hill	Anglo saxon burial site	SP 455613
Offchurch	Anglo saxon cemetery	SP 380655
Princethorpe	Anglo saxon burial site	SP 401703
St Neots	Anglo saxon cemetery	SP 188604
Stretton On Fosse	Anglo saxon domestic site	SP 218383
Warwick	Anglo saxon domestic site	SP 279648
Warwick	Anglo saxon cemetery	SP 275632
Wooten Wowen	Anglo saxon domestic site	SP152632

Discovering Saxon Sites

Ever since the earliest man walked the earth, the most important source was water. Infact this commodity determined whether man lived or died, water was so important to even the earliest of people that they believed there were water gods. People passing rivers springs and wells felt compelled to offer gifts to these gods in return that the water source would not dry up and would stay plentiful, the gifts ranged from swords & coins to family members in some circumstances although the last mentioned usually related to bog springs with the iron age and druidic peoples.

When the Saxons came to England, they had no problems finding water because the streams were already flowing with natural water and the Romans had already discovered most of the springs and underground wells. These were not hard to find because lots of them had villas built on them.

When the Romans left England the wells were there for the taking, It is a fact that the Romans chose the best of everything whilst they were here, this ranged from soils to settle on, fertile ground, also a good nearby water supply. Therefore it is not surprising that where the Romans have been, the Saxons have also been.

It is very important to note that there is a difference between Saxons visiting roman sites and losing stuff on those sites than Saxons actually settling on those sites, it is unusual for Saxons to actually settle on villa sites, Saxons mainly settled on adjouning fields. As this book contains the majority of sites already discovered, the information I am giving really concerns how to find new sites. I find that the best method of finding any Saxon site especially settlement is to compare modern survey maps to old ones, this way you can find wells and springs that are not listed on modern maps, you can also find original names of ancient fields on old maps which can point you to settlement or burials. As an example if there is a farm called little westfield, this tells me that there is some kind of settlement on a field west of the present farm. The main pointer to look for are farm names containing the word Ham, this is an early Saxon name which refers to early settlement, the ing or inga ham gives us the connection of early burial and settlement site.

When you come across a town or village containing the word ham but none of the farms contain no Saxon connection in their name then you should look for any connection with roman, this could prove that the roman site was the choice of the Saxons to settle on. It is also very important when researching farm names to find out if the name of that farm has been changed over the years, it could make all the difference to your research and save you lots of time, most farmers are proud to know the history of their land, if a farmer knows he has a saxon settlement on his farm and his farm is called say for example warham farm then he might change it to villa farm or to field house if he finds out there is also a villa on his land. for those of you who are new to the business, every farm name in England has a meaning and tells you what is on that farm. All farm names have been kept since the earliest of settlers and invaders arrived on our shores. As an example a farm called cold harbour tells us that romans where sheltering from the cold, probably a villa on a windy hill, then we have sober hill farm, a villa on a hill where the owner didn't drink, then we have red or whitehouse farms, usually the colours of villas that stood on the farms, or red house lane telling us that a red villa once stood on the lane. These names and many more are the same pointers concerning saxon named farms. Remember that those names are not there for the sake of it they mean something.

Soil Conditions

After carrying out research on numerous Saxon settlement and burial sites, especially on the Yorkshire wolds area, I found that 95% of those sites were on rich sandy gravels and chalk fields. I believe this due to good land drainage and fertile soils, obviously some parts of England do not contain gravels in the soil, if this being the case then when searching for sites, you should look for sandy soils, settlers looked for easy soils to dig into and to work, from experience, clay soils are a miss, it seems only the Georgians and Victorians were crazy enough to tackle clay, unless the clay was being used to make pottery.

Northampton

Abington	Anglo saxon burial site	SP 774613
Barton		
Seagrave	Anglo saxon cemetery	SP 887773
Brigstock	Anglo saxon domestic site	SP 945855
Brixworth	Anglo saxon cemetery	SP 747720
Brixworth	Anglo saxon cemetery	SP 744715
Brixworth	Anglo saxon Ind site	SP 751699
Cransley	Anglo saxon cemetery	SP 887773
Desborough	Anglo saxon cemetery	SP 805830
Duston	Anglo saxon cemetery	SP 726602

Ecton	Anglo saxon burial site	SP 830637
Far Cotton	Anglo saxon Ind site	SP 751603
Gt		
Addingham	Anglo saxon cemetery	SP 957744
Gt Oakley	Anglo saxon Ind site	SP 868845
Grendon	Anglo saxon burial site	SP 879604
Hackelton	Anglo saxon Ind site	SP 799558
Hardingstone	Anglo saxon burial site	SP 737583
Holdenby	Anglo saxon cemetery	SP 799558
Isham	Anglo saxon finds	SP 873744
Kettering	Anglo saxon cemetery	SP 876792

Milton	Anglo saxon burial site	SP 731552
Newton In Willows	Anglo saxon cemetery	SP 880833
Northampton	Anglo saxon Ind site	SP 749605
Pittsford	Anglo saxon cemetery	SP 747684
Rothwell	Anglo saxon cemetery	SP 815810
Rushton	Anglo saxon Ind site	SP 851826
Stanion	Anglo saxon Ind site	SP 90458593
St James end	Anglo saxon Ind site	SP 733585
Sudborough	Anglo saxon burial site	SP 967821
Thorpe Maisor	Anglo saxon cemetery	SP 832789

Thorpe

Waterville	**Anglo saxon Ind site**	**SP 018798**
Twywell	**Anglo saxon burial site**	**SP 937768**
Twywell Islip	**Anglo saxon cemetery**	**SP 980790**
Welford	**Anglo saxon brooch**	**SP 641803**
Welton	**Anglo saxon cemetery**	**SP 570664**
Woodford	**Anglo saxon burial site**	**SP 965765**

Berkshire

Abingdon	Anglo saxon burial sites	SU 501976
		SU 488975
	Anglo saxon cemetery	SU 490963
Arne Hill	Anglo saxon cemetery	SU 422872
Aston	Anglo saxon settlement	SU 784841
	Anglo saxon burial site	SU 783842
Blewburton Hill	Anglo saxon cemetery	SU 544861
Bray	Anglo saxon settlement	SU 918781
Britwell	Anglo saxon settlements	SU 950825
		SU 952825

Coleshill	Anglo saxon burial site	SU 237943
Cookham	Anglo saxon burial site	SU 886870
	Anglo saxon cemetery	SU 889858
Cranbourne	Anglo saxon burial site	SU 925728
	Grave goods	
Cross Barrows	Anglo saxon cemetery	SU 506810
Cook Hamsley	Anglo saxon burial site	SU 456850
Datchet	Anglo saxon coin hoard	SU 986758
E,Garston	Anglo saxon burial site	SU 358770
E.Shefford	Anglo saxon cemetery	SU 389749
Frilford	Anglo saxon burial site	SU 439962
	Anglo saxon cemetery	SU 437964
Harwell	Anglo saxon cemetery	SU 489882

Inkpen	Anglo saxon burial site	SU 349604
L.Wittenham	Anglo saxon cemeteries	SU 545937
		SU 540935
Lowbury	Anglo saxon burial site	SU 541823
Maidenhead	Anglo saxon settlement	SU 890812
Milton	Anglo saxon cemetery	SU 487925
Old Windsor	Anglo saxon settlement	SU 992746
Purley	Anglo saxon burial site	SU 654765
Radley	Anglo saxon domestic site	SU 513982
Reading	Anglo saxon burial sites	SU 725739
		SU 696720
	Anglo saxon cemetery	SU 698737

Sparsholt	Anglo saxon burial site	SU 348885
Stockholm Farm	Anglo – Viking burial site	SU 300885
Streatley	Anglo saxon burial site	SU 592812
Sutton Courtnay	Anglo saxon cemetery	SU 510945
	Anglo saxon burial site	SU 489940
Ufton Nervet	Anglo saxon domestic site	SU 617690
Upper Lambourne	Anglo saxon burial site	SU 328828
Upton	Anglo saxon settlement	SU 967800
	Anglo saxon burial site	SU 515868
Wallingford	Anglo saxon cemetery	SU 604890

Whistley

Green   **Anglo saxon settlement**   **SU 791745**

Wraysbury   **Anglo saxon settlement**   **SU 793742**

Wytham   **Anglo saxon cemetery**   **SU 474094**

Kent

Ash	Anglo saxon cemetery	TR 282582
Ashford	Anglo saxon cemetery	TR 010425
Aylesford	Anglo saxon cemetery	TQ 724583
Barham	Anglo saxon burial sites	TR 205485
		TR 202518
Beakersbourne	Anglo saxon cemetery	TR 207548
Betsham	Anglo saxon burial site	TQ 607715
Bifrons	Anglo saxon cemetery	TR 186552
Broughton Aluph	Anglo saxon burial site	TR 037487

Broadstairs	Anglo saxon cemetery	TR 375693
	Anglo saxon burial site	TR 393685
Buttsole	Anglo saxon cemetery	TR 311545
Canterbury	Anglo saxon domestic sites	TR 149575
		TR 150575
	Anglo saxon Ind site	TR 152576
	Anglo saxon burial site	TR 147570
Chartham	Anglo saxon cemetery	TR 108542
Chatham	Anglo saxon cemetery	TQ 764681
Coombe	Anglo saxon burial site	TR 298575
Darenth	Anglo saxon burial sites	TQ 531735
		TQ 566729
	Anglo saxon cemetery	TQ 566730

	Anglo saxon settlement	TQ 563706
	Anglo saxon domestic site	TQ 563508
Dartford	Anglo saxon domestic site	TQ 546746
Deal	Anglo saxon cemetery	TR 364508
Dover	Anglo saxon cemeteries	TR 238376
		TR 319414
East Bradbourne	Anglo saxon domestic site	TR 093417
Farningham	Anglo saxon cemetery	TQ 555665
Finglesham	Anglo saxon cemetery	TR 325534
	Anglo saxon burial site	TR 208380
Folkstone	Anglo saxon burial site	TR 230358

Freedown	**Anglo saxon burial site**	**TR 364470**
Gillingham	**Anglo saxon burial site**	**TQ 790687**
Gilton	**Anglo saxon cemetery**	**TR 281582**
Harrietsham	**Anglo saxon burial sites**	**TQ 874530**
		TQ 873536
Higham	**Anglo saxon cemetery**	**TQ 703736**
Holborough	**Anglo saxon cemetery**	**TQ 698626**
Hollingbourne	**Anglo saxon cemetery**	**TQ 821547**
Horton Kirkby	**Anglo saxon cemetery**	**TQ 564694**
Hoth	**Anglo saxon burial site**	**TR 204652**
Howletts	**Anglo saxon cemetery**	**TR 200568**

Littlebourne	Anglo saxon burial site	TR 906640
Hythe	Anglo saxon burial site	TR158350
Keston	Anglo saxon domestic site	TQ 415633
Kingston	Anglo saxon cemetery	TR 202519
Lenham	Anglo saxon burial sites	TQ 898521
		TQ 907526
Little Chart	Anglo saxon burial site	TQ 940457
Little Brook	Anglo saxon cemetery	TQ 556750
Little Halstow	Anglo saxon burial site	TQ 856665
Lullingstone	Anglo saxon burial site	TQ 533646
Lyminge	Anglo saxon cemeteries	TR 164407

		TR 163416
Lympne	Anglo saxon cemetery	TR 109349
Maidstone	Anglo saxon cemetery	TQ 736561
Manston	Anglo saxon cemetery	TR 355650
Margate	Anglo saxon cemeteries	TR349691
		TR 357708
Mersham	Anglo saxon burial site	TR 052393
Milton	Anglo saxon cemetery	TQ 910650
Monkton	Anglo saxon cemetery	TR 291655
Murston	Anglo saxon burial site	TQ 924646

Nethercourt Farm	Anglo saxon burial site	TR 366651
Northdown	Anglo saxon burial site	TR 380700
North Fleet	Anglo saxon cemetery	TQ 622738
Osengal	Anglo saxon burial site	TR 361654
Polhill	Anglo saxon cemetery	TR 505589
Reculver	Anglo saxon burial site	TR 200667
Ringwould	Anglo saxon burial site	TR 359483
Risely	Anglo saxon cemetery	TQ 562675
Rochester	Anglo saxon cemetery	TQ 747680
Santum	Anglo saxon domestic site	TR 120340

Sarre	Anglo saxon cemetery	TR 261650
Shelford Farm	Anglo saxon burial site	TR 164602
Sibertswold	Anglo saxon cemetery	TR 266488
Snodland	Anglo saxon cemetery	TR 701627
Southfleet	Anglo saxon cemetery	TQ 617726
Staneshill	Anglo saxon burial site	TR 190612
Stowting	Anglo saxon cemetery	TR 123423
Strood	Anglo saxon burial site	TQ 687732
		TQ720672
		TQ 729691
Temple Ewell	Anglo saxon cemetery	TR 291443

Teynham	Anglo saxon cemetery	TQ 956637
Thurnham	Anglo saxon cemetery	TQ 806578
Upchurch	Anglo saxon cemetery	TQ 828671
Westwell	Anglo saxon burial site	TQ 990474
Wickhambreux	Anglo saxon burial site	TR 226603
Wingham	Anglo saxon cemetery	TR 249569
Woodnesborough	Anglo saxon jewellery	TR 308568
Worth	Anglo saxon burial site	TR 337553
Wrotham	Anglo saxon burial site	TQ 619590
		TQ 615598
Wye	Anglo saxon cemeteries	TR 070465
		TR 069470

Essex

Beauchamp	Anglo saxon domestic site	TQ 762937
Birdbrook	Anglo saxon burial site	TL 715424
Broomfield	Anglo saxon burial site	TL 710096
Bulmer	Anglo saxon domestic site	TL 828387
Chadwell St Mary	Anglo saxon domestic site	TQ 657779
Colchester	Anglo saxon cemetery & Domestic site	TL 997250
Feering	Anglo saxon cemetery	TL 868192
Gestingthorpe	Anglo saxon domestic site	TL 834385

Gt Chesterford	Anglo saxon cemeteries	TL 501435
		TL 502434
		TL 503429
Gt Dunmow	Anglo saxon domestic site	TL 626219
Heybridge	Anglo saxon domestic site	TL 850082
	Anglo saxon burial site	TL 855081
Kelvedon	Anglo saxon cemetery	TL 867191
Maldon	Anglo saxon domestic site	TL 851070
N.Stifford	Anglo saxon Ind site	TQ 600800
L.Oakley	Anglo saxon domestic site	TM 222292
Plum Berow	Anglo saxon burial site	TQ 840938
Prittlewell	Anglo saxon cemetery	TQ 878873

Rainham	Anglo saxon cemetery	TQ 554840
Rivenhall	Anglo saxon domestic site	TL 828178
Saffron Walden	Anglo saxon cemetery	TL 535382
Thurrock	Anglo saxon cemetery	TQ 651805
Village Not Researched	Prolific finds from this site	TL 553838
Waltham Abbey	Anglo saxon Ind site	TL 380007
	Anglo saxon domestic site	TL 381007
Wendens Ambo	Anglo saxon domestic site	TL 510365
	Anglo saxon burial site	TL 518363
Wicken Bonhunt	Anglo saxon domestic site	TL 511335
Witham	Anglo saxon burial site	TL 818151

Prospective Sites

As we now know that nearly all settlers made their homes near to wells, streams, rivers and springs. it is now very important to remember that when searching for those Saxon sites we must first take a look at the surrounding landsape. we know from research that the Saxons didn't like the wind, this meant finding lowland fields which were flat or gentally sloping surrounded by hills, preferably valley bottoms/dales, this would have offered lots of comfort and protection against all kinds of ailments.

The fields we need to look for would be those which have adjoining natural streams which have steep banks, the reason being that these streams would not have risen much so would not have flooded any settlement nearby, the contant running of these waters make it impossible for the waters to rise, when rain hits the water it flows away. still water rivers and certain streams tend to rise and flood.

The romans certainly knew this and so did the Saxons, when taking all this into account we must now look for good workable settlement soils for drainage/crops, our thinking methods today are much the same as theirs were back then, good places to search are between old villages near boundaries and [adding the information from above] if you can stick to this then your chances of finding these sites are very high.

In east Yorkshire I have looked at lots of discovered settlement sites and have noticed that most are set in the above conditions which are already outlined above. the only differences being that some Saxon sites stand alone on their own with no other sites near to them, others are on adjouning fields with a field separating them.

Most of these Saxon settlements stand near to roman roads and or villa sites but never on those sites, either standing just off the Roman roads/villa sites or just a handful of fields away, looking at these Saxon settlement patterns it looks like they were a very private peoples and liked to keep to themselves and didn't like to intrude on anyone else, this must be true due to settlement patterns showing one site on one field then no other for at least a couple of miles, with the Romans it was usually a villa or settlement of some kind every half mile to a mile, always in view of each other incase help was needed, the Anglians/Saxons were a very choosy race of people indeed and were very clever and particular.

Gloucestershire

Bourton On Water	Anglo saxon domestic site	SP 171221
Broadwell	Anglo saxon burial site	SP 192271
Burn Ground	Anglo saxon burial site	SP 100156
Chavenage	Anglo saxon burial site	SP 877960
Cirencester	Anglo saxon burial site	SP 016023
Fairford	Anglo saxon cemeteries	SP 145015
		SP 146014
Foxcote Manor	Anglo saxon burial site	SP 012180
Gloucester	Anglo saxon Ind sites	SO 820188
		SO 820186

Hidcote

Bartrim   Anglo saxon burial site   SP 175428

Kemble   Anglo saxon cemeteries   ST 971966

                                            SP 989978

Kempsford Anglo saxon burial site   SU 155974

Leckhampton

Hill   Anglo saxon burial site   SO 946186

Oddington Anglo saxon cemetery   SP 216253

Poulton   Anglo saxon burial site   SP 105045

Salmonsbury Anglo saxon cemetery   SP 177204

Upper Swell Anglo saxon burial sites   SP 167263

                                            SP 171265

Upton   Anglo saxon domestic site   SP 152344

Derbyshire

Alsop	Anglo saxon burial site	SK 163553
Barton Blount	Anglo saxon domestic site	SK 209346
Benty grange	Anglo saxon burial site	SK 146642
Bore low	Anglo saxon burial site	SK 179977
Borrowash	Anglo saxon burial site	SK 414342
Bowers low	Anglo saxon burial site	SK 169526
Brushfield	Anglo saxon burial site	SK 166717
Calver low	Anglo saxon burial site	SK 236745
Chelmorton	Anglo saxon burial sites	SK 128626
		SK 118694

Cold heaton	Anglo saxon burial site	SK 148567
Cow lowe	Anglo saxon burial site	SK 102730
Galley lowe	Anglo saxon burial site	SK 214564
Grind law	Anglo saxon burial site	SK 200673
Hurdlow	Anglo saxon burial site	SK 117666
Kings newton	Anglo saxon cemetery	SK 390260
Middleton	Anglo saxon burial site	SK 187615
Monsal dale	Anglo saxon burial site	SK 178723
Pilsbury	Anglo saxon burial site	SK 120639
Sharp low	Anglo saxon burial site	SK 161528

Stand low	Anglo saxon burial site	SK 159534
Swarkeston	Anglo saxon cemetery	SK 365295
Tissington	Anglo saxon burial site	SK 153267
Vincent knoll	Anglo saxon burial site	SK 137635
Waggon low	Anglo saxon burial site	SK 115648
White low	Anglo saxon burial site	SK 225598
Willington	Anglo saxon domestic site	SK 287277
Wyaston	Anglo saxon burial site	SK 195424

Hampshire

Alresford	Anglo saxon burial site	SU 589313
Alton	Anglo saxon cemetery	SU 715387
Bedhampton	Anglo saxon burial site	SU 692064
Bishops Waltham	Anglo saxon domestic site	SU 553175
Bournmouth	Anglo saxon burial site	SZ 138933
Brockbridge	Anglo saxon Ind site	SU 600180
Broughton Down	Anglo saxon burial site	SU 307316
Buriton	Anglo saxon Ind site	SU 738201

Chalton	Anglo saxon Ind site	SU 730170
Chilbolton	Anglo saxon burial site	SU 384390
	Anglo saxon domestic site	SU 384390
Corhampton	Anglo saxon Ind site	SU 618209
Cupernham	Anglo saxon Ind site	SU351211
Droxford	Anglo saxon cemetery	SU 612184
Emsworth	Anglo saxon domestic site	SU 746054
Fareham	Anglo saxon burial site	SU 575065
Farley Chamberlayne	Anglo saxon burial site	SU 403286
Kings somborne	Anglo saxon Ind site	SU 361310

Kings worthy	Anglo saxon cemetery	SU 499329
Micheldever	Anglo saxon cemetery	SU 505396
Middle Wallop	Anglo saxon burial site	SU 290378
Milton	Anglo saxon burial site	SZ 238941
Never wallop	Anglo saxon burial site	SU 304364
Northam	Anglo saxon Ind sites	SU 420110
		SU 424122
		SU 420115
Nursling	Anglo saxon burial site	SU 359169
Portsdown hill	Anglo saxon cemeteries	SU 667064
		SU 648066
Preshaw	Anglo saxon burial site	SU 580240

Preston Candover	**Anglo saxon burial site**	**SU 604403**
Shipton Bellinger	**Anglo saxon burial site**	**SU 232446**
Snells corner	**Anglo saxon cemetery**	**SU 707153**
Stoke charity	**Anglo saxon Ind site**	**SU 490386**
Sutton scotney	**Anglo saxon burial site**	**SU 462391**
Wallington	**Anglo saxon burial site**	**SU 590075**
W.Ham	**Anglo saxon burial site**	**SU624519**
Winchester	**Anglo saxon cemetery**	**SU 494293**
West hill	**Anglo saxon burial site**	**SU 472295**
Winnall	**Anglo saxon burial sites**	**SU 491301**
		SU 494301

Barrow burials [Secondaries]

Throughout England there are thousands of barrow sites which are scattered across our landscape, long, round & bowl and termed as tumuli or tumulus, these date from the iron age, bronze age & Neolithic periods, in many of these ancient barrows there have been phenomenal numbers of Anglian/Anglo Saxon internment burials round the sides of these mounds, they consist of cremations & burials.

Nobody knows the reasons why these people chose such places to bury their dead, maybe it was the fact that these large mounds stood out like landmarks so that the families of their dead would always be able to find them, they probably also knew that these mounds would still be stood there thousands of years later, there is also the belief that due to being virtually 75-80% buried nearly stood up, these people could walk into their afterlife out of the barrow.

In places like the Yorkshire wolds, there are literally hundreds upon hundreds of these barrows blotted on the landscape, some fields only have one barrow in them, some contain a couple then others contain large clusters of them, some totally ploughed down or out through modern farming methods.

Large numbers of barrows still remain prominent on the wolds and are easily recognizable, whatever their status most of them were excavated and found to contain burials and cremations, the grave goods included jewellery with gold along with coins, artefacts and other relics.

Some burials classed as minor, others major and classed of national importance, the latter usually listed as monumental sites/heritage and are fenced off to stop the mounds being damaged, some of these sites are also classed as henges where people worshipped.

After reading all Mortimer and Greenwell reports on these excavations, I was surprised to see only a few of the graves contained sceattas.

From the majority of these excavations items such as tweezers,buckles,clasps,rings,bangles,girdlehangers,brooch es,keys,knives,spearheads and lots of other goods but no coins, it makes me wonder if the pagan people had turned to Christianity long before people believed they had, could they have had the same beliefs as Christians today that you can't take riches into the afterlife? you cant buy your way to the gods, was it that they just gave it to their love ones to use?

From reading these excavation papers and talking to many other fellow Detectorists who detect Saxon sites,I learned that you don't usually find sceattas on ploughed out barrows which contain Saxon/Anglian burials, coins are only usually found on adjacent settlement fields, or if there has been plenty of activity near those barrows, I cant say if this is true or false because ive not detected on barrow sites, also the fact that the detecting business is like the secret society, only a man who gives up detecting for life might tell you where there is a barrow full of sceattas, these coins are much sought after and trying to find them is like trying to find a needle in a haystack.

Everyone knows through reading reports or through detecting on barrows that they produce little or nothing and the only finds that turn up are the odd bits of Roman, some barrows do produce Saxon goods like pins/strapends, if you find these items on any site then theres a 90% chance that you will find sceattas kicking about somewhere in the soil.

Finding these sceattas is another matter, you can swing your machine just that bit to fast and you could have walked over dozens of these tiny coins not knowing they are there.

As an example I went onto a large Saxon settlement site three years ago which was supposed to have been cleaned out years ago, the group of detectorists who used to do it gave it up as a dead loss, I got permission and went on the site with my Sceat Busting Explorer II, nearly every 20 feet bang bang bang bang, sceattas deep down in black sandy soil everywhere, over the 3 years up to date Explorer II had weaned out over 170 sceattas from that one site.

If you have not yet found a sceatta and are getting frustrated like most do, then you have to stand back and ask yourself a few questions, are you using the right machine for the job? are you using the machine properly? are you on a settlement site? have sceattas been found on the site before? has the site been thoroughly and truly cleaned out? if there is nothing on the site then you wont find nothing, don't give up on a site that has produced good stuff then its gone barren, there are many sites like this that stop producing then a couple of years later start to give up lots of new stuff.

Cremation Cemeteries

Sancton Anglian cremation cemetery in E.Yorkshire is probably amongst one of the largest of its kind in England

There were over 700 cremation urns found on the north by east end of a large filled in chalk pit, this cemetery was investigated following reports of urns being found in 1873, excavations were carried out not long after by Greenwell, Rolleston and others including hull museum many years later in 1954-57, the site was a wealth of early Anglian pottery, metalwork and a multitude of small finds.

Once again whilst reading reports on cremation cemeteries excavated, hardly any grave goods had been listed from any of these cremation cemeteries, 90% of them seemed to be void of goods, therefore the burials at Sancton must have been very important for there to be so many goods buried with those urns, I had spoken to a Detectorist who was one of the first on the site in the 1970s, he told me that from the high end of the field he had found a large number of beautiful long and square headed brooches, he had also found many sceattas, as I know the man to be very honest and reliable I have no reason to doubt him.

I will now revert back to barrow barrows, how is it that the cremation and skeleton flat burial cemeteries are producing goods in every way when barrow burials produce very little? some of these barrows are prolific but the majority are very poor concerning goods, especially sceattas.

Concerning the above cemetery, you would think that there had to be some kind of very large settlement nearby for so many burials? there are no settlements of any kind in the close vicinity connected with that cemetery, how do I know? well I have thoroughly detected nearly every field within 10 sq miles of that site over a 15 year period and have not found any settlement connected to that site.

We have to assume that these urns for some very important reason where carted to that specific site from miles around to be buried in that location but why? nearly all those cremations dated to the same period so that means hundreds of Anglians died all of a sudden within a short space of time of each other, we have to ask this question, did those hundreds of Anglians wish to be cremated or buried? where their wishes ignored? if none of those burials were cremations, that would of meant carting hundreds of bodies to the site then having to dig hundreds of deep holes to put those bodies into, where they cremated because it was a lot easier to move urns than bodies? its a very hard question to answer.

Due to there being no nearby settlement for which those people came from, it proves that those urns were taken there from all over the place, or that a full Anglian village had been wiped out, if that's the case then why wern't they buried in the place they came from or died at? it is fact in most cases that were there are burials there is settlement nearby especially where the Anglians/Saxons are concerned and that is part of why they are known as the dark ages

Bedfordshire

Astwick	Anglo saxon cemetery	TL 216385
Bedford	Anglo saxon domestic site	TL 053597
Clifton	Anglo saxon burial site & Grave goods	TL 169388
Cross hall	Anglo saxon burial site	TL 173615
Dunstable	Anglo saxon cemetery	TL 006210
	Anglo saxon domestic site	TL 003235
Dyers hill farm	Anglo saxon burial site	TL 042180
Eaton ford	Anglo saxon Ind site	TL 160580
	Anglo saxon village	TL 17335890
Easton socon	Anglo saxon burial site	TL 172603

Eggington	Anglo saxon burial site	SP 960254
Elstow	Anglo saxon Ind site	TL 040460
Eynesbury		
Conygeer	Anglo saxon burial site	SP 188595
Fancot	Anglo saxon burial site	TL 018279
Felmersham	Anglo saxon domestic site	SP 990578
Harrold	Anglo saxon cemetery	SP 954572
Harrowden	Anglo saxon burial site	TL 069471
Kempston	Anglo saxon cemetery	TL 031474
Leighton Buzzard	Anglo saxon cemeteries	SP 921265

		SP 928262
Limbury	Anglo saxon burial site	TL 065246
Luton	Anglo saxon cemetery	TL 081229
	Anglo saxon burial sites	TL 081215
		TL 065238
Moggerhanger	Anglo saxon burial site	TL 134850
Pegsdon Common	Anglo saxon burial site	TL 133310
Puddle hill	Anglo saxon cemetery	TL 004234
Ravensden	Anglo saxon burial site	TL 078544

Gtr London

Bromley	**Anglo saxon cemetery**	**TQ 467675**
Holborn	**Anglo saxon Ind sites**	**TQ 301811**
		TQ 303807
		TQ 304811
		TQ 304808
Savoy	**Anglo saxon domestic site**	**TQ 300799**
Shoreditch	**Anglo saxon Ind site**	**TQ 325811**
Whitehall	**Anglo saxon domestic site**	**TQ 300799**

Buckinghamshire

Ashendon	Anglo saxon burial site	SP 705142
Bishopstone	Anglo saxon cemetery	SP 799110
Bledow	Anglo saxon burial site	SP 775014
	Anglo saxon cemetery	SP 774101
Dinton	Anglo saxon cemetery	SP 765114
Ellesborough	Anglo saxon burial site	SP 845070
Eythorpe	Anglo saxon burial site	SP 771141
High Wycombe	Anglo saxon burial site	SU 866931
Hitcham	Anglo saxon burial site	SU 921811
Latimer	Anglo saxon domestic site	SU 998986

Mentmore	Anglo saxon cemetery	SP 906196
Newport		
Pagnell	Anglo saxon cemeteries	SP 863448
		SP 887433
Stone	Anglo saxon cemetery	SP 779122
	Anglo saxon burial site	SP 807110
Taplow	Anglo saxon burial site	SU 906821

Hereford & Worcestershire

Beckford	**Anglo saxon burial sites**	**SO 964355**
		SO 969355
Blockley	**Anglo saxon burial site**	**SP 184369**
Brickle Hampton	**Anglo saxon burial site**	**SO 982412**
Broadway	**Anglo saxon burial site**	**SP 118369**
Fladbury	**Anglo saxon domestic site**	**SO 996464**
Hereford	**Anglo saxon domestic site**	**SO 508404**
Ipsey	**Anglo saxon domestic site**	**SP 067666**
Little Hampton	**Anglo saxon burial site**	**SP 026432**

Upton sndsbury Anglo saxon burial site   SO 944544

Wyre piddle   Anglo saxon burial site   SO 061473

Durham & Hertford

Castle eden	Anglo saxon burial site	NZ 427385
Cornforth	Anglo saxon burial site	NZ 313329
Darlington	Anglo saxon cemetery	NZ 286150
Ettersgill	Anglo saxon Ind site	NY 888277
Hartlepool	Anglo saxon cemetery	NZ 530335
Houghton le Spring	Anglo saxon burial site	NZ 353492

Ashwell	Anglo saxon burial site	TL 298386
Furneux Pelham	Anglo saxon burial site	TL 440269
Kings walden	Anglo saxon burial site	TL 140220
Pirton	Anglo saxon burial site	TL 138311
Therfield	Anglo saxon domestic site	TL 340403
	Anglo saxon burial site	TL 335373

Leicestershire

Bagworth	Anglo saxon Ind sites	SK 439062
		SK 442065
Beeby	Anglo saxon burial site	SK 636098
Breedon on The hill	Anglo saxon burial site	SK 404233
Caldecot	Anglo saxon settlement	SP 851935
Cotesbach	Anglo saxon burial site	SP 524819
Cottesmore	Anglo saxon burial site	SP 902136
Empingham	Anglo saxon cemeteries	SK 944077
		SK 936082
		SK 942080
Glaston	Anglo saxon settlement	SK 896005

Glen parva	Anglo saxon cemetery	SP 569987
Goadby	Anglo saxon settlement & Strapends found	SK 779266
Gt Bowden	Anglo saxon settlement	SP 744888
Gt Casterton	Anglo saxon settlement	TF 001092
	Anglo saxon burial site	TF 002093
Harston	Anglo saxon domestic site	SK 850314
Husbands Bosworth	Anglo saxon burial site	SP 648836
Ingarsby	Anglo saxon burial site	SK 685053
Ketton	Anglo saxon settlement & cemetery	SK 969056

Kirkby bellars	Anglo saxon domestic site	SK 718183
Kirkdale close	Anglo saxon burial site	SK 823311
Langham	Anglo saxon settlements	SK 858102
Little Casterton	Anglo saxon Ind site	TF 000095
Loughborough	Anglo saxon burial site	SK 535195
Mkt overton	Anglo saxon cemeteries	SK 887176
Melbourne	Anglo saxon settlement &	SP 798930
	Burials with cemetery	SP 794932
Melton Morbray	Anglo saxon cemetery	SK 756194

N Luffenham	Anglo saxon cemetery	SK 932045
Rothley temple	Anglo saxon burial site	SK 568122
Rowley fields	Anglo saxon cemetery	SK 571019
Seaton	Anglo saxon cemetery	SP 904983
Slawston	Anglo saxon settlement	SP 790936
Stoke golding	Anglo saxon burial site	SP 396970
Sysonby	Anglo saxon cemetery	SP 738189
Thurmaston	Anglo saxon cemetery	SK 617084
Tickencote	Anglo saxon settlements	SK 985093
Twyford	Anglo saxon cemetery	SK 730101

Wanlip	Anglo saxon settlement &	SK 596103
	Burials & cemetery	SK 596108
Westcotes	Anglo saxon cemetery	SK 574032
Wigston magna	Anglo saxon cemetery	SP 608978

Staffordshire

Calton	Anglo saxon burial site	SK 108502
Castern Llam	Anglo saxon burial site	SK 123526
Catholm	Anglo saxon domestic site	SK 203175
	Extensive saxon village	
	Found in 1973	SK 197164
Littleworth	Anglo saxon Ind site	SJ 921232
Musden	Anglo saxon burial sites	SK 116501
		SK 118500
Stapenhill	Anglo saxon cemetery	SK 257212
Steep Lowe	Anglo saxon burial site	SK 123561
Stone rural	Anglo saxon settlement	SJ 875366

Stretton	Anglo saxon cemetery	SK 253263
Tamworth	Anglo saxon domestic sites	SK 207041
		SK 208041
	Anglo saxon cemetery & Ind site	SK 200040
Wetton	Anglo saxon burial site	SK 118547
Wichnor	Anglo saxon burial site	SK 194159

Proof Of Anglian/Saxon Settlement

How do you know if you are on an Anglian or Saxon settlement site? the answer is that you don't know unless that site has already been excavated, reports kept and published, yourself and/or the other Detectorists have discovered numerous items on that site, even though that site might have proved productive, it still does not prove settlement, we have to remember that certain cemeteries throughout England have also proved very productive leading to probable settlement beliefs.

Over a 20 year period I have detected on a large number of burial sites and have found some very nice girdle hangers and cruciform brooches.

I have also found mounts,buckles,spindle whorls and other nice stuff, due to what I was finding I believed I was on settlement sites until the farmers informed me that they were cemeteries & burial sites, I have found that on actual settlement sites most of these produce large amounts of tiny rock solid lead pieces, usually amongst this lot or nearby you start to find the pins, stykas and sceattas with strapends and other stuff.

When first investigating any prospective Saxon site, you should never hope to find any Anglian/Saxon pottery, there just seems to be very little of it or none at all on most of the sites, I don't know if this is due to fieldwalkers removing it or reasons unknown, or maybe the Saxons found it much easier to use roman pottery due to the vast amounts left behind when they departed?

The most probable sites to find Saxon/Anglian pottery are on cremation sites not settlement, so where does that leave us concerning the finding of new & undiscovered sites? believe me you wont find anything on the surface of a field unless you are very lucky, that being the case then how do we find these sites? [Ref to discovering Saxon sites]

From my own experiences it is better to start at a site which has already been discovered [Grid Refs In This Book] then spend all your spare time detecting all the adjoining fields, remember though that you must first get permission from the landowner, that to me is the easy part, finding sceattas and other stuff is much harder, you can talk to a farmer but you cant talk to a field, we can all go out detecting and find endless hammereds, roman coins, brooches & other common stuff but not Saxon , they just didn't seem to leave much trace of where they settled for some reason.

If you are new or relatively new in the detecting business, if you take up hunting Saxon then you must learn to be very patient and committed to what you are searching for, if not then you will be very disappointed, some detectorists are very lucky, they just plod onto the field, swing their machine like a 9 iron on a golf course then walk off the field with a lovely Saxon coin or artefact.

Others spend weeks, months, years without luck or the item they find is sadly broken, I think most of us have experienced this at some time or other and it can be very depressing.

If you are struggling to get land permission or you are not finding any Saxon coins or artefacts, then you should speak to other detectorists/and or historians because you can gain valuable information concerning old villages and sites that you didn't know about, even though lots of detectorists are cagey about giving site information away which is understandable, there are lots of them who will help you out so you can get started, historians love to talk to anyone concerning the history of their village or town because they are proud of it, the information they give you is usually very reliable, most local vicars can also give you valuable information too, many of them have records relating to the village and the church, these can go back to the dark ages, libraries also keep good stocks of reference books, you can also visit the museum or council archives department but remember that there is normally a charge and time limit.

If it all sounds too much effort or you feel as though you are struggling, then either way I advise you to find out where your local detector club is and join that, most of these have set limits regarding numbers but they vary, one of the advantages of joining a club is that most of the research gets done by the sites officer who gains land permission on behalf of the club, whatever your choice this book I have written has put you right in at the top where you need to be, most of the sites listed will probably produce some form of coin/artefact but like I said you have to get permission to detect on that land.

My experiences of the farming community have not been too bad as far as detecting permission goes, I find that if you talk to the farmer as though you have known him for years then you've cracked it, when I approach a farmer I already know about the history of his farm, I also know about the farming business too,I start off by casually walking up to the farmer then ill smile and say good morning boss hows business goin not too bad I hope, I now have the farmers attention, how can I help you? i now say that I am a detectorist and I would appreciate just a few minutes of his time, farmers are all different, at this point some will say im not interested or I have already got someone who does it, if this is the case then take him at his word and thank him anyway, don't ramble on and annoy him.

I find that most like to talk though, even so on the above example, ask the farmer if you can give him your details incase the other detectorists give up on his land, tell him you would be greatful if he could contact you back at a later date, going back to me getting the farmers attention, I wonder if it would be possible to have a go on your Saxon settlement or villa field with my metal detector? i will share all finds with you, it would be great to give you something historical from your land, most farmers have grandchildren who one day might inherit the farm or who will run it, wouldn't it be great to give something to the grandkids? i find most farmers who were not interested when first approached are now interested in what im saying to them, well I suppose you could have a day on it then to see how things go, remember that in reality we all know that things are not perfect concerning disclosing finds to farmers, anyone who believes otherwise are on another planet.

Lots of farmers are paranoid which is only understandable under the circumstances, they have either had bad experiences in the past with detectorists or they feel as they cant trust you as what they don't know about on their land they cant miss, they wouldn't like to know that a hoard of gold coins had vanished from under their feet just because they had a detectorist on their land, if they knew the scenario in advance then they would rather the hoard had stayed where it was to save stress, this is only an example but things like this have happened and do exist as we all know.

There are some very important factors involved in detecting concerning permission, as an example there are many differences concerning the interpretation of words and laws, if the farmer told me that I could detect his land and I could keep whatever I find for free or for £20, in effect the farmer might have been very silly to say that incase a found a million pound hoard, under this scenario it is best to get a written agreement were you both sign it, otherwise you might run into lots of problems, the farmer might believe that there is genuinely nothing on his land and so has made the above statement, as soon as something very valuable got put under his nose then he would change his tune.

My landlord was a farmer and also a businessman, he would chase a penny down a drain to retrieve it, farmers are very clever where money is concerned so if ever confronted with the above offer get it on paper, its in your best interests, there is a difference between getting permission to detect and retrieving finds from the land, permission to detect does not permit the right to retrieve finds from the land, when you ask for permission make sure you ask the landowner if the detecting includes digging and retrieval of items, most detectorists and farmers are quite sensible and can always reach a verbal agreement or understanding concerning most scenarios but there are others on both sides who end up going through the courts so remember the advise, you might need it when you don't expect it.

I find it a good thing to read the farmers weekly so it keeps me up to date with the talk of the day amongst farmers, you would feel very silly and embarrassed if you said to the farmer I see the price of beet is the best its ever been, the farmer then says hes just lost five grand on his crop, you must know what you are talking about or you wont make many friends amongst the farmers, remember they are a tight knit community and they are always chatting amongst themselves whether on the phone, radio, or in the farmers arms pub, some days I stand talking to farmers for up to 3 hours in the farmyard, it goes from detecting to the price of hay through to the agricultural minister, some days I don't get any detecting done.

I suppose I had been lucky by having a farmer landlord, the fact that I had always been a good painter too helped with certain aspects, I completed the first farmers house and he stood back in amazement, it wasn't long before the other farmers were contacting me to do work for them, its things like this that build trust between yourself and the farming community, basically you just turn up with your machine and your on the land, I have lots of farmers who just say to me you know you've got the run of the land, this is a great thing but you can also end up with too much land, up to date I can have permission on 26 farms and have more acreage than lord bath, I did start off with more farms but gave some away to detectorists who were struggling for permission, I have been detecting since 1997 and have hardly touched any of the above land, this is due to good finds on the first few farms which have kept me on those, also with crops being constantly in and out you just don't know where you are with it all.

I can accept is can be very hard to gain permission and stating the above might annoy a few people but at the end of the day I have done my research and have used up years of my life gaining what ive got, if you don't try or ask then you don't get.

Surrey

Ashtead	Anglo saxon burial sites	TQ 200573
		TQ 182567
Banstead	Anglo saxon cemeteries	T Q 243582
		TQ 241612
		TQ 247612
Carshalton	Anglo saxon burial site	TQ 270642
Chean	Anglo saxon burial site	TQ 375585
Cobham	Anglo saxon burial site	TQ 114602
Coulsdon	Anglo saxon burial sites	TQ 300574
		TQ 299583
		TQ 312624
		TQ 299580
	Anglo saxon cemetery	TQ 291587

E.Horsley	Anglo saxon burial site	TQ 095528
Effingham	Anglo saxon burial site	TQ 111529
Esher	Anglo saxon burial site	TQ 139650
Ewell	Anglo saxon burial sites	TQ 219622
		TQ 219621
		TQ 219623
Farnham	Anglo saxon domestic site	SU 842466
Fetcham	Anglo saxon burial sites	TQ 160567
		TQ 156554
		TQ 159561
	Anglo saxon settlement	TQ 157562
Guilford	Anglo saxon burial site	SU 992429
Guildown	Anglo saxon cemetery	SU 988488

Merrow	Anglo saxon burial site	TQ 029502
Norney	Anglo saxon settlement	SU 943437
Reigate	Anglo saxon cemetery	TQ 238500
Sanderstead	Anglo saxon burial site	TQ 331624
Shepperton Green	Anglo saxon settlement & Domestic site	TQ 070676
Tadworth	Anglo saxon cemetery	TQ 229577
Worplesden	Anglo saxon burial site	SU 991537

Sussex

Alfriston	**Anglo saxon cemetery**	**TQ 516037**
	Prolific finds site	
Birling gap	**Anglo saxon cemetery**	**TV 595008**
Bishopstone	**Anglo saxon settlement**	**TQ 468009**
	Anglo saxon domestic site	**TQ 468007**
Black patch	**Anglo saxon burial site**	**TQ 094088**
Brighton	**Anglo saxon cemetery**	**TQ 303056**
Burpham	**Anglo saxon domestic site**	**TQ 039086**
Clayton	**Anglo saxon burial site**	**TQ 304133**
Coombs	**Anglo saxon burial site**	**TQ 182084**
Earls down	**Anglo saxon Ind site**	**TQ 637197**

E.Chiltington	Anglo saxon burial site	TQ 370125
Eastbourne	Anglo saxon burial site	TV 602998
Firle	Anglo saxon burial site	TQ 488057
Friston hill	Anglo saxon burial site	TV 545991
Glynde	Anglo saxon settlement	TQ 445104
	Anglo saxon burial sites	TQ 460084
		TQ 449111
Hammond Place	Anglo saxon burial site	TQ 307185
Hamsey	Anglo saxon burial site	TQ 392119
Hangleton	Anglo saxon burial site	TQ 262073
Hassocks	Anglo saxon burial site	TQ 296115

Highdown	Anglo saxon cemetery	TQ 092043
Hodshrove	Anglo saxon burial site	TQ 329069
Lewes	Anglo saxon burial site	TQ 407095
Malling hill	Anglo saxon burial site	TQ 421112
Medmerry	Anglo saxon domestic site	SZ 837937
Ocklynge hill	Anglo saxon burial site	TQ 595007
Old Shoreham	Anglo saxon cemetery	TQ 204075
Peppering	Anglo saxon burial site	TQ 044106
Perry hill	Anglo saxon burial site	TQ 055094
Portslade	Anglo saxon burial site	TQ 259052

Rodmell	Anglo saxon burial site	TQ 413053
Rottingdean	Anglo saxon burial site	TQ 371054
Saddlescoombe	Anglo saxon burial site	TQ 270111
Selmeston	Anglo saxon burial site	TQ 558072
Shoreham	Anglo saxon burial site	TQ 214065
Southese	Anglo saxon burial site	TQ 423053
Stanmer	Anglo saxon cemetery	TQ 328101
Steyning	Anglo saxon domestic site	TQ 214051
	Anglo saxon Ind site	TQ 178114
	Anglo saxon burial site	TQ 168103
	Anglo saxon settlement	TQ 175111
Sullington hill	Anglo saxon burial site	TQ 094120

Telscombe	Anglo saxon domestic site	TQ 405033
Thakenham	Anglo saxon domestic site	TQ 104174
West stoke	Anglo saxon burial site	SU 820098
Wolstonbury Hill	Anglo saxon burial site	TQ 284138
Woodingdean	Anglo saxon cemetery	TQ 365054

Wiltshire

Alton priors	Anglo saxon settlement	SU 107620
Alvediston	Anglo saxon burial site	ST 967252
Amesbury	Anglo saxon burial site	SU119427
Ashton valley	Anglo saxon burial sites	ST 979426
		ST 980428
Avebury	Anglo saxon settlement	SU 099696
Barrow hill	Anglo saxon burial site	ST 993234
Bassett down	Anglo saxon burial site	SU 115199
Boscombe	Anglo saxon burial site	SU 177400
Bowls barrow	Anglo saxon burial site	ST 942467

Broad chalke	Anglo saxon cemetery	SU 042250
Broad town	Anglo saxon burial site	SU 090772
Callas hill	Anglo saxon burial site	SU 215830
Calne	Anglo saxon burial site	ST 999709
Chippenham	Anglo saxon settlement	ST 898727
Clarendon	Anglo saxon cemetery	SU 163293
Cold harbour	Anglo saxon Ind site	
	Gold coin found	ST 871451
Durrington	Anglo saxon burial site	SU 116441
E.Grafton	Anglo saxon burial site	SU 293600
Elston	Anglo saxon burial site	SU 073513

Everley	Anglo saxon burial site	ST 184560
Fargo	Anglo saxon cemetery	SU 275689
Filands	Anglo saxon Ind site	ST 932872
Foxhill	Anglo saxon cemetery	SU 223822
Gomeldon	Anglo saxon cemetery	SU 182352
Gt bedwyn	Anglo saxon burial site	SU 261623
Harnham hill	Anglo saxon cemetery	SU 137387
Heytesbury	Anglo saxon burial site	ST 920428
Hilperton Marsh	Anglo saxon Ind site	ST 854578

Hinton down	Anglo saxon burial site	SU 253800
Kemble	Anglo saxon burial site	ST 987972
Kill barrow	Anglo saxon burial site	ST 006479
Kings p down	Anglo saxon burial site	SU 009659
Knook	Anglo saxon burial site	ST 956446
Laverstock	Anglo saxon cemetery	SU 156293
	Anglo saxon settlement	SU156293
Lechlade	Anglo saxon settlement	SU 212374
Little down	Anglo saxon burial site	SU 133374
Lopcoombe Corner	Anglo saxon cemetery	
	Reputed warrior graves	SU 250357

Lower

Everleigh	Anglo saxon settlement	SU 175534
Marlborough	Anglo saxon burial site	SU 207686
Mildenhall	Anglo saxon burial site	SU 210697
Netheravon	Anglo saxon burial site	SY 156486
New town	Anglo saxon Ind site	SU 272715

Ogbourne St

Andrews	Anglo saxon burial site	SU 188723
Perham down	Anglo saxon burial site	SU 246494
Purton	Anglo saxon cemetery	SU 108874
Sherrington	Anglo saxon burial site	ST 968391

Stanton Fitzwarren	**Anglo saxon burial sites**	**SU 188905**
		SU 160901
Swindon	**Anglo saxon burial site**	**SU 158831**
Temple Down	**Anglo saxon burial site**	**SU 135727**
Tilshead Lodge	**Anglo saxon burial site**	**SU 021475**
Trowbridge	**Anglo saxon settlement**	**ST 855759**
Walcot	**Anglo saxon settlements**	**SU 159837**
		SU 158837
Warminster	**Anglo saxon burial site**	**ST 885456**
W.Chisenbury	**Anglo saxon burial site**	**SU 136531**

W.Kennet	Anglo saxon burial site	SU 119683
W.Knoyle	Anglo saxon burial sites	ST 863337
		ST 863357
W.Overton	Anglo saxon settlement	ST 132699
Westbury	Anglo saxon domestic site	ST 873503
Winklebury		
Hill	Anglo saxon cemeteries	ST 951212
		ST 950212
Winterbourne		
Gunner	Anglo saxon cemetery	SU 182352
Winterbourne		
Stoke	Anglo saxon burial sites	SU 076420
		SU 104422

SU 101416

Winterslow	Anglo saxon burial sites	SU 234348
		SU 228353
Witherington	Anglo saxon burial site	SU 185252
Yatesbury	Anglo saxon burial site	SU 070709

Oxfordshire

Benson	Anglo saxon burial site	SU 615908
Black bourton	Anglo saxon burial site	SP 286041
Brighthampton	Anglo saxon cemetery	SP 383033
Brize Norton	Anglo saxon burial sites	SP 300091
		SP 305082
Broughton Poggs	Anglo saxon cemetery	SP 221043
Burford	Anglo saxon burial site	SP 247120
Cassington	Anglo saxon domestic sites	SP 444124
		SP 453103

	Anglo saxon cemeteries	SP 443116
		SP 450102
		SP 457210
Chadlington	Anglo saxon cemetery	SP 330210
Chinnor	Anglo saxon burial sites	SP 751001
		SP 765002
Clifton		
Hampden	Anglo saxon burial site	SU 544960
Cokethorpe	Anglo saxon burial site	SP 375060
Cuddesdon	Anglo saxon cemetery	SP 599032
Ducklington	Anglo saxon burial site	SP 360076
East hundred	Anglo saxon cemetery	SU 248991

Ewelme	**Anglo saxon cemetery**	**SU 645927**
Eynsham	**Anglo saxon domestic sites**	**SP 430108**
	Anglo saxon cemetery	**SP 436098**
Filkins	**Anglo saxon cemetery**	**SP 237043**
Headington	**Anglo saxon burial site**	**SP 550079**
Heyford Purcell	**Anglo saxon cemetery**	**SP 488245**
Hordley	**Anglo saxon domestic site**	**SP 445187**
Hornton	**Anglo saxon burial site**	**SP 392450**
Idbury	**Anglo saxon burial site**	**SP 226195**
Kidlington	**Anglo saxon burial site**	**SP 497148**

Kinsey	Anglo saxon burial site	SP 741072
Kirtlington	Anglo saxon burial site	SP 499203
Lyneham	Anglo saxon cemetery	SP 297210
Minster Lovell	Anglo saxon burial site	SP 317110
New wintles	Anglo saxon domestic site	SP 432108
New Yatt	Anglo saxon Ind site	SP 374238
North leigh	Anglo saxon cemetery	SP 378143
Oddington	Anglo saxon cemetery	SP 553152
Osney	Anglo saxon burial site	SP 501060
Oxford	Anglo saxon domestic site	SP 512078

Shackenoak	Anglo saxon domestic site	SP 373138
Souldern	Anglo saxoN burial site	SP 519314
Spelsbury	Anglo saxon domestic site	SP 339213
	Anglo saxon finds	SP 351218
Standlake	Anglo saxon domestic site	SP 385045
	Anglo saxon cemetery	SP 386046
Stanton Harcourt	Anglo saxon domestic site	SP 403055
	Anglo saxon cemetery	SP 411051
Tadmarton	Anglo saxon burial site	SP 393378
Upper Heyford	Anglo saxon burial site	SP 521256
Wallingford	Anglo saxon domestic site	SU 608898
Watchfield	Anglo saxon cemeteries	SU 249908
		SU 249908
Wheatley	Anglo saxon cemetery	SP 602046

The Dark Age

It is common knowledge that concerning the dark ages we know very little about our ancestor the Saxons,for centuries historians and archaeologists have struggled to find the answers concerning the above race of people.

Very little or nothing was known about the Saxons as far back as the 17th century, the odd skeleton ploughed up by the oxen or the odd brooch or ornament found, this only confirmed that the items where old and unusual nothing more.

It wasn't until certain people became interested in history and their past that oddments or blots on the landscape like barrows were dug into, during these digs skeletons were discovered, some with treasure and some with little or nothing, this still gave no information as to whom the people were or why they were buried inside a remote lonely hill on a field, it was only after word got around concerning these barrow burials that people started excavating them all over Britain, 'after all' these barrows stood out like a sore thumb so were very easy to find.

Due to there being lots of poor people in the late Tudor and Georgian periods, these barrows became an easy target for thieves and opportunists, it was no different to when the tombs were being robbed in Egypt, it became a race against time for the Archaeologist to excavate as many barrows as possible before they were robbed and valuable information lost forever, back then they did not have the laws we have now to protect these sites so it became a free for all for anyone who wished to dig in.

It is very important to note that in the county of East Yorkshire and the wolds, nearly every bronze age barrow was excavated by an Archaeologist named Mortimer, he excavated these barrows over a forty year period and he put his life and soul into the job, Greenwell also worked with Mortimer on many of these sites, they started their work in the late 1850s and fully recorded every dig in detail, the pair also investigated flat cemeteries, these two became so important in their time that lots of other Archaeologists often turned to them for advise and direction, Mortimer also compiled reports on behalf of other archaeologist doing digs.

After reading many of Mortimers reports on his excavations, the only problem he encountered was that he could not state if the penannular brooch was Roman or Saxon, these brooches often turned up in Saxon graves and could not be identified as being from one or the other period, it was known that the Romans had them before the Saxons, but it is believed that the early Saxons continued to wear them so they are hard to date, it is accepted that the brooches overlapped from one period to the other.

Early Kingship Period

The Germanic or early Anglo Saxon peoples as we know them first settled in what we call England in the fifth and sixth centuries, they formed their own tiny kingdoms throughout England, in the year 450 the Roman empire was suffering with lots of problems on the continent, this was due to the tribes of the Vandals,Burgundians,Alaric and the Visigoths who had penetrated the Rhine into Gaul [Roman territory] this lead the Romans to abandon Britain, this opened the door for barbarian attackers from Ireland, the Picts from Scotland and the Saxons from Germany.

Before the above period had escalated, Saxons from the North German area had already visited Britain as pirates or mercenaries, during the break up of the Roman provincies it is believed that many of them were later ruled by a king called Vortigern during the mid fifth century, it is said that Vortigern raised a powerful force of Saxon mercenaries which were lead by Hengest and Horsa, these mercenaries turned on Vortigern then formed a kingdom of their own which we know as being kent.

It wasn't long before ship loads of settlers left Germany where they sailed up the Thames,Wash and Humber, even though the native Britons were quite strong, they were still conquered then tiny confederations were set up, during the sixth century it is believed that a hero named Arthur drove the German invaders out of the South Midlands, by the late sixth century it is said that everything was taken back by the invaders who went on to conquer most of England.

These invaders were known as the Angles,Saxons, and Jutes, the Saxons came from Northern Germany known as [Old Saxony] the Angles came from the border of North Germany and Denmark, the Jutes probably came from Friesland or Rhineland, whilst these invaders gathered together in England they often acted very roughly, the angles stayed in the north and midlands while the Saxons were in the south and west, the jutes stayed in kent and Hampshire.

It was by the year 600 that the Saxons had established their kingdoms and had settled firmly in England, leading kingdoms had emerged where the chief being Northumbria which was the most powerful of the seventh century, this was later challenged by Mercia who took over in the eighth, Wessex later took over in the ninth century.

Pagan & Conversion

During the early period from the 450s to the mid seventh century, the invaders were what you would call pagan, they worshipped their own idols and false gods, one of these gods is known as Woden, it was only through much hard work and persistence of missionaries from Christian Ireland and Rome along with Wales and Scotland that the conversion to Christianity took place.

In the year 600, St Augustine from Rome began his conversion of the English followed later by the English Christian church being firmly established, in the seventh century, a pope by the name of Theodore of Tarsus sent a Syrian Greek to be the Archbishop of Canterbury, by the eighth century Venerable Bede came on the scene and the English church was at the centre of western civilisation.

Then the Danes arrived in England to ruin all the good work that had been done, they Raped, Robbed, Murdered, and burned the English church to the ground, after all, these invaders were pagan and had no respect for Englands new found church and their god, by 871 the Danes had conquered most of England which was now ruled by king Alfred, when he later died, his son Edward the elder took over followed by his grandson Athelstan, then by his great grandson Edgar, they laid peaceful foundations until the later Danes under Swein raided again in 1013.

Afterword

Over the years since I first started detecting, I discovered like everyone else that there was some kind of barrier between the Detectorist and the Archaeologist,I have read and hear about so many different stories from both sides of the argument, infact I have been involved in a few myself, it is important that I remain impartial because I don't like to discuss individual cases, I believe that the barriers can only be removed in certain cases when certain individuals change their attitude towards each other. A lot of the problem does lie within the system itself and not with the individual Detectorist or Archaeologist,

Rules, regulations and certain laws have to be followed even if we they are wrong and not fair, everybody acts and thinks differently, what one person thinks is right the next thinks its wrong, whether it be the treasure act, recording schemes, declaring finds or being refused requested information on sites or any other relevant matter.

We all have our own views and beliefs on those matters, at the end of the day, Detectorists will do what they choose to do, Archaeologist will do likewise so where is the problem? disagreements and grievances are not the end of the world so get that detector out and find that treasure before it rots in the ground, keep promoting the good of the hobby and carry on recording those finds.

Bibliography

East Yorkshire & Wolds

Mortimer & Greenwell papers 1905

C & E Grantham papers 1955

Beresford & Hirst papers 1971

Lincolnshire

Dudley papers 1949

Myers papers 1951

Meaney papers 1964

Philips papers 1954

Thompson papers 1956

[Anglo Saxon Sites In Lincolnshire]

Pevsner papers 1964

Brown papers 1906

Riley papers 1957

Manby papers 1964

Fowler papers 1968

Mortimer/40 years research in saxon burial mounds in east Yorkshire

Mary Clark/bracelet & toilet set

[burton fields farm gravel pit]

1938-43 [Leeds philosophical & literary society]

Anglian & settlement patterns in Yorkshire [Faul 1974]

Warwick & Staffs/Midlands

Victor Skipp/The centre of England 1979 [p97-106]

Catholme/Wychnor/Barton/London/Excellent book

Norfolk/Suffolk/Cambridge

John Seymour/Guide to East Anglia 1970

Many References for Saxon towns & Villages [Excellent]

Wiltshire [Archaeological & Natural history Mag 61 [1966]

Gloucester/Donovan & Dunning 1936

Saxon burials at Foxcote Manor

D.B Harden/Dark Age Britain 1956

Meaney/Agazetteer of early Anglo Saxon Burial Sites [1964]

Myres/The Angles/The Saxons/The Jutes [1970[

Stenton/Anglo Saxon England [1947] 2nd Edition Oxford

Wessex D.J Bonney/Early Boundaries in Wessex [In P.J

Fowler 1972]

Please note that all site entries/Grid Refs and other information have been very carefully checked and researched over a 12 months period, over 100 archaeological journals have been read,many archive visits and many various searches on archaeological sites on the internet, and all cross referenced in order to compile this book.